Contents

Unit 5: When Fall Comes

Meets **Accreditation Standard** for **Child-created Bulletin Boards**

Unit 7: Author Study—Eric Carle

Unit 6: It's Pumpkin Pickin' Time

Introduction

This series of monthly activity books is designed to give PreK and Kindergarten teachers a collection of hands-on activities and ideas for each month of the year. The activities are standards-based and reflect the philosophy that children learn best through play. The teacher can use these ideas to enhance the development of language and math skills, and of social/emotional and physical growth of children. The opportunity to promote pre-reading skills is present throughout the series and should be incorporated whenever possible.

Organization and Features

Each book consists of seven units:

Unit 1 provides reproducible pages and information for the month in general.
- a newsletter outline to promote parent communication
- a blank thematic border page
- a list of special days in the month
- calendar ideas to promote math skills
- a blank calendar grid that can also be used as an incentive chart

Units 2–6 include an array of activities for five **theme** topics. Each unit includes
- teacher information on the theme
- arts and crafts ideas
- a food activity
- poetry, songs, and books
- bulletin board ideas
- center activities correlated to specific learning standards

Implement the activities in a way that best meets the needs of individual children.

Unit 7 focuses on a well-known **children's author**. The unit includes
- a biography of the author
- activities based on a literature selection
- a list of books by the author
- reproducible bookmarks

In addition, each book contains
- reproducible **icons** suitable to use as labels for centers in the classroom. The icons coordinate with the centers in the book. They may also be used with a work assignment chart to aid in assigning children to centers.
- reproducible **student awards**
- **calendar day pattern** with suggested activities

Research Base

Howard Gardner's theory of multiple intelligences, or learning styles, validates teaching thematically and using a variety of approaches to help children learn. Providing a variety of experiences will assure that each child has an opportunity to learn in a comfortable way.

Following are the learning styles identified by Howard Gardner.
- **Verbal/Linguistic** learners need opportunities to read, listen, write, learn new words, and tell stories.
- **Bodily/Kinesthetic** learners learn best through physical activities.
- **Musical** learners enjoy music activities.
- **Logical/Mathematical** learners need opportunities to problem solve, count, measure, and do patterning activities.
- **Visual/Spatial** learners need opportunities to paint, draw, sculpt, and create artworks.
- **Interpersonal** learners benefit from group discussions and group projects.
- **Intrapersonal** learners learn best in solitary activities, such as reading, writing in journals, and reflecting on information.
- **Naturalist** learners need opportunities to observe weather and nature and to take care of animals and plants.
- **Existential** learners can be fostered in the early years by asking children to think and respond, by discussions, and by writing.

Gardner, H. (1994). *Frames of mind*. New York: Basic Books.

October News

Teacher:_____ Date:_____

Headline News

Coming Up

Happy Birthday to

Special Thanks to

Help Wanted

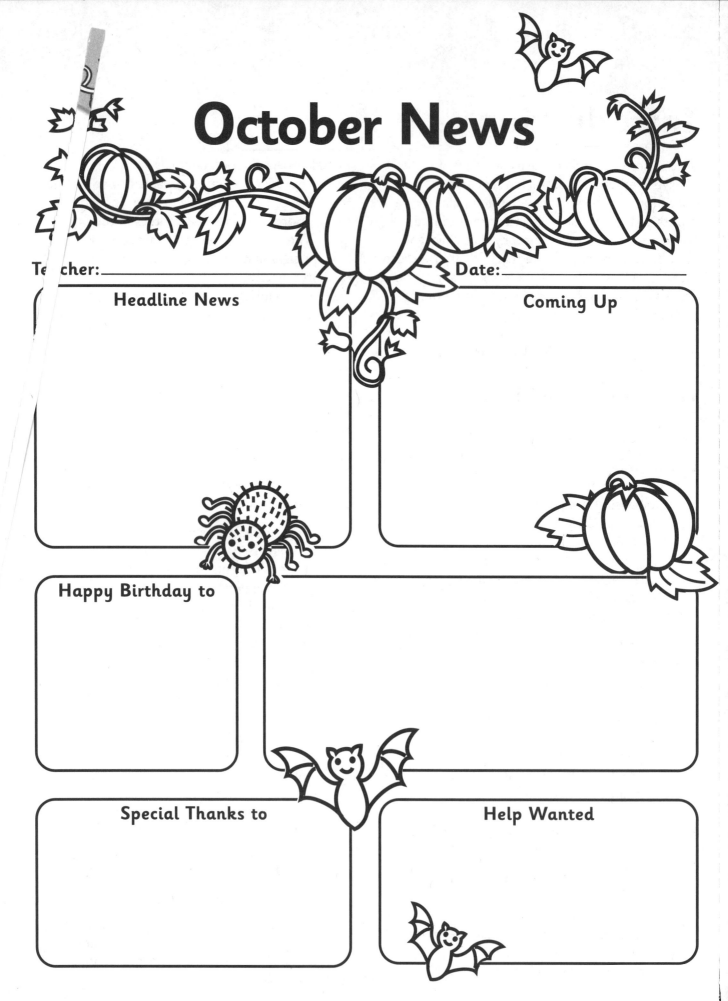

Three Cheers for October PreK–K, SV 9829-9

October

Three Cheers for October PreK–K, SV 9829-9

Special Days in October

Fire Prevention Month Read *The Story of Smokey Bear* by Robin Bromley (Dutton Books) and lead a discussion about fire safety. During the month of October, guide children in planning and executing a fire drill.

National Pasta Month  Prepare a variety of different shaped pasta. Mix with a sauce and have children eat pasta for a snack. Provide uncooked pasta for center activities, such as sorting, making patterns, or creating artwork.

Red Ribbon Week Participate in the National Drug Awareness program and lead a discussion with children about saying no to drugs. Have children wear sneakers to school on a designated day and make a sign that says, "We run away from drugs."

2 Farm Animals Day Invite children to sing "Old MacDonald Had a Farm" and include as many farm animals as possible.

5 World Teacher's Day Have children write or dictate a sentence about what they think is the most important thing that a teacher does. Invite them to draw a picture of their teacher.

9 Count's Birthday on Sesame Street Read a book about the Count. Provide children with a handful of small objects and have them count how many they have.

11 Columbus Day Display a picture of Columbus and the three ships. Lead a discussion about how people thought the world was flat. Have children follow the path of his voyage on a globe.

12 Farmer's Day Add farmer's clothes and animal masks to the dramatic play center. Invite children to role-play being a farmer.

14 Grover's Birthday on Sesame Street Read a story about Grover. Then have children make a birthday card for him. Invite them to draw a picture of Grover on the card.

16 Dictionary Day Make a list of several words that are of interest to children. Demonstrate how to find the meaning of those words by looking in the dictionary. Write the meaning of each word on a chart.

20 National Fruit Day Use the recipe on page 12 of the Bat unit to make fruit kabobs. Have children taste other unusual fruits such as kiwis or mangos.

22 National Nut Day Check for allergies before touching or tasting nuts. Have children sort nuts by size, shape, or kind. Then crack open the nuts and taste different kinds.

25 Pablo Picasso (1881) Introduce children to Picasso's art with either a book or the Internet. Make a graph and record which children like his paintings and which do not. Have them give a reason for their choice.

28 Statue of Liberty Dedicated (1886) Display a picture of the Statue of Liberty. Have children make their own torch with a paper towel tube and tissue paper.

31 Halloween Celebrated Have children do activities from the It's Pumpkin Pickin' Time unit beginning on page 71.

Three Cheers for October PreK–K, SV 9829-9

October

Sunday	Monday	Tuesday	Wednesday	Thursday	Friday	Saturday

Unit 1, Teacher Resources: October Calendar
Three Cheers for October PreK–K, SV 9829-9

Calendar Activities for October

Classroom Calendar Setup

The use of the calendar in the classroom can provide children with daily practice in learning days, weeks, months, and years. As you plan the setup for your classroom, include enough space on the wall to staple a calendar grid labeled with the days of the week. Leave space above the grid for the name of the month and the year. Next to the calendar, staple twelve cards labeled with the months of the year and the number of days in each month. Leave these items on the wall all year. At the beginning of each month, start with the blank calendar grid. Do not staple anything on the grid that refers to the new month. Leave the days of the week and the year in place.

Introducing the Month of October

Before children arrive, gather all of the items that will go on the calendar for October. You may want to include the following:
- name of the month
- number cards
- name cards to indicate birthdays during the month
- picture cards that tell about special holidays or school events during the month
- a small treat to be taped on the day of each child's birthday. You may wish to gift-wrap the treat.

Add a special pointer that can be used each day while doing calendar activities. See page 9 for directions on how to make a pointer. Place these items in a picnic basket. Select a puppet that can remain in the basket and come out only to bring items for each new month. A dog puppet works well because of the large mouth, which makes it easier to grasp each item.

On the first school day of the month, follow this procedure:
1. Place the picnic basket in front of the class. Pull out the puppet and introduce it to children if it is the first time they have seen it or ask them if they remember why the puppet is here. If this is the first time they have seen it, explain that the puppet will visit on the first day of each month to bring the new calendar items.
2. Have the puppet pull out the name of the month. According to the abilities of children, have them name the first letter in the name of the month, count the letters, or find the vowels. Staple the name of the month above the calendar.
3. Have the puppet pull out the new pointer for the teacher or the daily helper to use each day during calendar time.
4. Next, pull out the number cards for October. You may use plain number cards, cards made from the calendar day pattern on page 96, or seasonal die-cut shapes. By using two or three die-cut shapes, you can incorporate building patterns as part of your daily calendar routine. See page 9 for pattern ideas.

5. Place the number one card or die-cut under the day of the week on which October begins. Locate October on the month cards that are stapled next to your calendar. Have children tell how many days this month will have and then count that many spaces on the calendar to indicate the end of the month. You may wish to place a small stop sign as a visual reminder of the end of the month. Save the remaining numbers cards or die-cut shapes and add one each day.

6. If there are any birthdays during October, have the puppet pull out of the basket the cards that have a birthday symbol with the child's name and birth date written on it. Count from the number 1 to find where to staple these as a visual reminder of each child's birthday. If you have included a wrapped treat for each child, tape it on the calendar on the correct day.

7. Finally, have the puppet bring out cards that have pictures of holidays or special happenings, such as field trips, picture day, or story time in the library. Staple the picture cards on the correct day on the calendar grid. You can use these to practice various counting skills, such as counting how many days until a field trip, a birthday, or a holiday.

8. When the basket is empty, say goodbye to the puppet and return it to the picnic basket. Put the basket away until the next month. Children will look forward to the beginning of each month in order to see what items the puppet will bring for the class calendar.

Making a Spider Pointer

Include a spider pointer in the calendar basket for this month. To make a pointer, you will need the following:

- two 2" black pom-poms
- four black chenille stems
- a medium-sized dowel rod that is 18" long
- several 12" lengths of narrow black and orange ribbon
- florist wire or tape

Directions:

1. Hot-glue the ribbons to the end of the dowel rod so that they lie against the rod.
2. Hot-glue the two pom-poms together to make the spider's body.
3. Cut the chenille stems in half and hot-glue them to one side of the pom-poms. Bend the stems to look like eight legs.
4. Tie the spider to the end of the dowel rod with a piece of florist tape or wire.

The calendar helper can use this to point to the day of the week, the number, the month, and the year as the class says the date each day.

Patterning

Practice patterning by writing the numbers 1–31 on two different die-cut shapes, such as a bat and a pumpkin. Write the numbers on the shapes in order using an AABBAABB pattern. Each day have the helper add a die-cut shape to the calendar. Challenge children to predict the shape for the next day.

Going Batty over Bats

 Over 1,000 species of bats live on every continent of the world, except Antarctica.

 The largest bats live in warm areas, and smaller bats live in both warm and cold places. In regions that have cold winters, bats migrate to warmer climates or hibernate.

 Bats that hibernate gather in large groups and sleep close together for warmth.

 Bats are mammals that are covered with fur. Bats have live babies that drink milk from the mother's body. They are the only mammal that can fly.

 Bats are nocturnal and sleep upside down. They use the claws on their feet to grasp onto a twig or the interior of a cave and hang close together.

 Most female bats have one baby at a time. Baby bats are called pups. At birth, the pup has no hair, and its eyes are closed.

 A pup clings to its mother and drinks her milk until it is old enough to fly. Most bats in the United States learn to fly in two to five weeks.

 Bats have teeth and chew their food. Seventy percent of all bats eat insects.

 Bats use their wings to catch insects. Their wings are covered with a tough skin and no hair. Their wings have little thumbs on them and are used like hands.

 A single bat can eat up to 1,000 insects an hour and is, therefore, a great help to people. Fruit and nectar-eating bats are also very helpful because they are among the most important seed dispersers and pollinators.

 Some bats eat mice, frogs, and fish. They use echolocation to find their food in the dark.

 Many people fear bats because of rabies. Actually, only one-half of 1 percent of all bats have rabies. It is wise to use caution around bats as with all wild animals. However, bats are a very valuable part of the world's ecosystem.

A Bat Hat

Materials

- patterns on page 19
- sentence strips
- brown or black construction paper
- scissors
- glue
- stapler
- wiggly eyes
- pencils

Directions

Teacher Preparation: Duplicate the head and wing pattern to use as a template. Enlarge the patterns, if desired.

1. Trace and cut out a head and two wings on brown or black construction paper.

2. Glue the bat head to the middle of the sentence strip.

3. Glue two wiggly eyes on the bat head.

4. Fold the tab on the bat wings and staple the wings to the sides of the sentence strip.

5. Staple the sentence strip to form a headband. Adjust the band to fit each child's head.

Baby Bat Finger Puppet

Materials

- patterns on page 20
- crayons or markers
- scissors
- glue

Directions

Teacher Preparation: Duplicate a copy of the bat and finger puppet for each child.

1. Color and cut out the bat and finger puppet patterns.

2. Glue the bat to the center of the finger puppet.

3. Glue the ends of the finger puppet together. Adjust to fit child's finger.

Extension: Make a set of five finger puppets and use with the song on page 13.

Three Cheers for October PreK–K, SV 9829-9

Bat Fruit Kabobs

You will need

- banana slices
- pineapple chunks
- grape halves
- cantaloupe chunks
- straws
- picture of a fruit bat

Directions

Teacher Preparation: Cut fruit into bite-size pieces.

Lead a discussion with children about fruit bats and how they help with seed dispersal.

1. Fill a straw with fruit pieces.
2. Go "batty" over this sweet treat!

Three Cheers for October PreK–K, SV 9829-9

🎵 Five Little Bats

(Tune: "Five Little Snowmen")

Five little bats are we

Hanging upside down in a tree.

One flew away in the dark, dark night.

What a sight to see!

Four little bats are we

Hanging upside down in a tree.

One flew away in the dark, dark night.

What a sight to see!

Have children repeat the verses, counting down to one.
Have children sing the song and use the finger puppets
made in "Baby Bat Finger Puppet" on page 11.

Books to Go Batty Over

Bats
by Gail Gibbons (Holiday House)

Bats Around the Clock
by Kathi Appelt (HarperCollins)

Bats: Creatures of the Night
by Joyce Milton (Grosset & Dunlap)

Bat Jamboree
by Kathi Appelt (HarperTrophy)

Beautiful Bats
by Linda Glaser (Millbrook Press)

Stellaluna
by Janell Cannon (Harcourt Children's Books)

Three Cheers for October PreK–K, SV 9829-9

The Bat Cave

Materials

- patterns on page 20
- brown craft paper
- black construction paper
- black tempera paint
- paintbrushes
- border
- empty bathroom tissue rolls
- stapler
- glue
- scissors
- wiggly eyes

Directions

Teacher Preparation: Duplicate the head and feet patterns to use as a template. Crumple brown craft paper and staple to the bulletin board so that it looks like the inside of a cave. Trace and cut out each child's handprints on black construction paper. Provide each child with two handprints.

1. Press one end of an empty roll flat and then cut a point to resemble a short bat tail. Paint the roll black.

2. Overlap handprints and glue on the back of the tissue roll for the bat wings.

3. Trace the head and feet templates on the black paper and cut them out.

4. Glue wiggly eyes on the head and then glue the head onto the tissue roll. Glue the feet to the end with the point.

5. Staple the bats upside down in a pleasing arrangement on the bulletin board.

6. Add a border and the caption.

Three Cheers for October PreK–K, SV 9829-9

Going Batty over Bats Centers

Art Center

Science Standard
Understands characteristics of organisms

Bats in a Cave

Materials

- blue construction paper
- paintbrushes
- glue
- brown tempera paint
- bat-shaped confetti
- crayons

Lead a discussion with children about bats. Discuss how they are nocturnal and hunt for food at night. Some bats live in caves with thousands of other bats. Invite children to paint a cave on the blue construction paper. Then have them glue several pieces of the bat-shaped confetti next to the cave. Encourage children to draw a night scene in the background.

Dramatic Play Center

Science Standard
Understands characteristics of organisms

Come to the Bat Cave

Materials

- appliance box
- paintbrushes
- bat masks
- black tempera paint
- several yards of black fabric

Teacher Preparation: Cut fabric into pieces that children can use as bat wings. Purchase plastic bat masks at a discount store. Cut one end off of the box so that it looks like a cave.

Invite children to paint bats hanging upside down on the inside of the box. Have them wear the masks and stretch the fabric across their backs and arms like wings. Then have them role-play bats flying in and out of the cave.

Going Batty over Bats Centers

Game Center

Social Studies Standard
Follows rules such as taking turns

Echoing Sounds

Materials

- scarf
- rhythm sticks

Lead a discussion with children about how some bats use echolocation to find insects in the dark. The bats cannot see the insects but the bats' ears catch the sounds that the insects make.

Have partners play this game. Cover one child's eyes with the scarf. Then have the partner move away and make a sound with the rhythm sticks. Have the blindfolded partner listen for the sound and point in the direction from which the sound came. Invite partners to exchange materials and repeat the game.

Language Center

Language Arts Standard
Recognizes rhyming words

Sounds Like "Bat"

Materials

- patterns on page 21
- crayons
- scissors

Teacher Preparation: Duplicate, color, and cut out the patterns. Cut the slits on the bat. Pull the letter strip through the slits.

Invite children to pull the strip and read each new word that rhymes with *bat*.

Going Batty over Bats Centers

Math Center

Math Standard
Associates numerals with sets of objects

Count the Bats

Materials

- activity master on page 22
- pencil
- crayons

Teacher Preparation: Duplicate a copy of the activity master for each child.

Invite children to count the bats. Then have them circle the number that tells how many.

Reading Center

Language Arts Standard
Distinguishes words in sentences

Read the Sentence

Materials

- cards on page 23
- flannel board
- construction paper
- sentence strips
- scissors
- small felt squares
- glue

Teacher Preparation: Duplicate the word cards on construction paper and cut them apart. Write *Bats fly at night.* and *They are mammals.* on sentence strips. Glue a small square of felt on the back of each word card and each sentence strip for flannel board use.

Have each child choose a sentence strip and place it on the flannel board. Then have the child place the word cards below the sentence strip, matching the word order. Ask the child to point to each word and read the sentence.

Going Batty over Bats Centers

Science Center

Math Standard
Sorts or classifies objects by kind

What's for Dinner?

Materials

- pictures of different types of bats
- plastic insects
- plastic fruit
- plastic fish or frogs

Display the pictures of different bats. Then lead a discussion about how bats have different food sources. Some eat fruit, some eat insects, and others eat fish or frogs. Invite children to sort the items according to what each kind of bat would eat.

Note: Vampire bats do lap blood from animals such as cows or chickens. However, this information may not be appropriate for younger children.

Writing Center

Language Arts Standard
Makes illustrations to match sentences

What Did Baby Bat See?

Materials

- activity master on page 24
- pencil
- crayons

Teacher Preparation: Duplicate a copy of the activity master for each child.

Lead a discussion with children about nocturnal animals. They, like bats, sleep during the day and hunt for food at night. Invite children to draw a picture of something a baby bat might see if it flew out of a cave during the day. Then have them write or dictate an answer to complete the sentence.

Bat Head and Wing Patterns

Use with "A Bat Hat" on page 11.

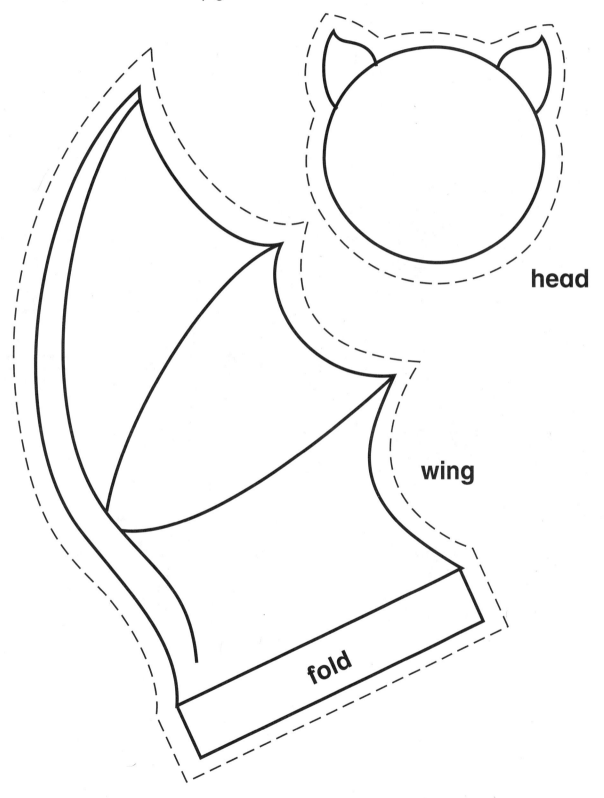

head

wing

fold

Three Cheers for October PreK–K, SV 9829-9

Bat Finger Puppet Patterns

Use with "Baby Bat Finger Puppet" on page 11.

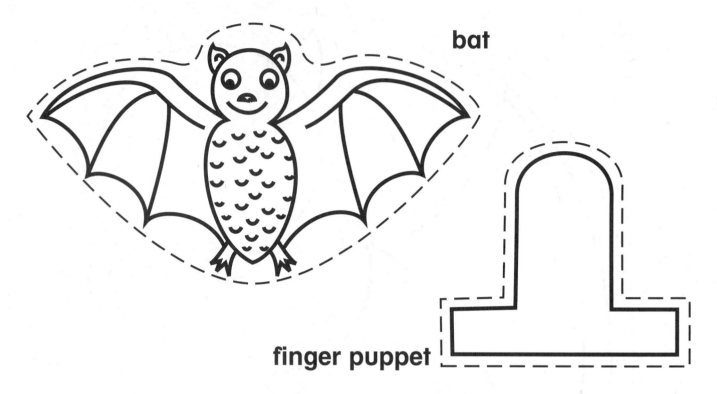

bat

finger puppet

Bat Head and Feet Patterns

Use with "The Bat Cave" on page 14.

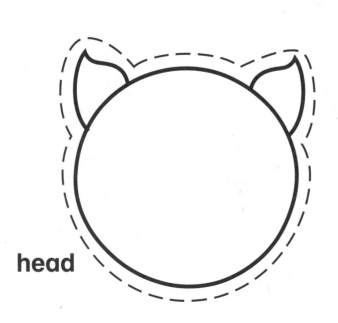

head

feet

Three Cheers for October PreK–K, SV 9829-9

Rhyming Words Patterns

Use with "Sounds Like 'Bat'" on page 16.

Three Cheers for October PreK–K, SV 9829-9

Counting

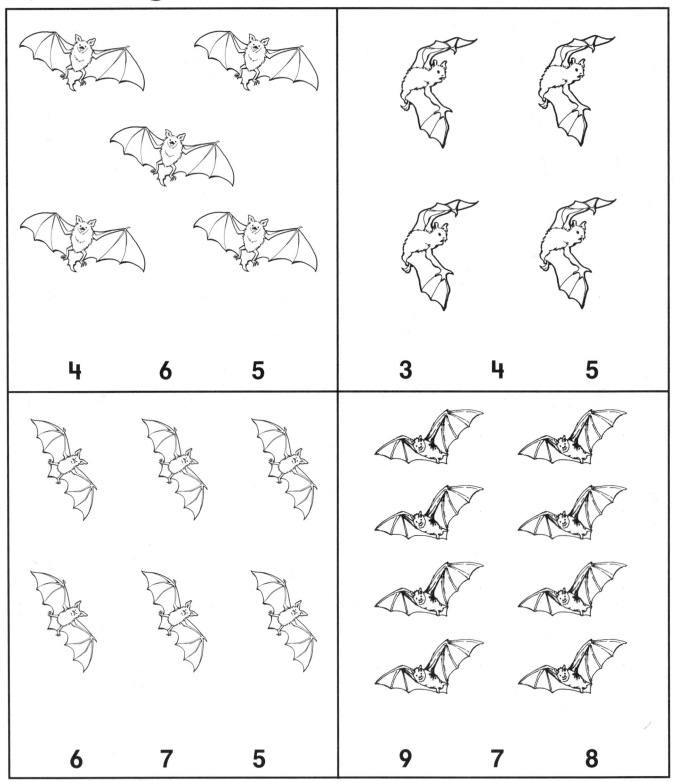

4   6   5

3   4   5

6   7   5

9   7   8

Directions: Use with "Count the Bats" on page 17. Invite children to count the bats. Then have them circle the number that tells how many.

Unit 2, Going Batty over Bats: Activity Master
Three Cheers for October PreK–K, SV 9829-9

Word Cards

Use with "Read the Sentence" on page 17.

at

fly

Bats

They

night.

mammals.

are

Name _____

Things to See During the Day

One day Baby Bat flew out and saw

_____

_____

_____

_____.

Directions: Use with "What Did Baby Bat See?" on page 18. Invite children to draw a picture of something a baby bat might see during the day if it flew out of a cave. Then have them write or dictate an answer to complete the sentence.

Bony Old Skeletons

Mammals, birds, reptiles, amphibians, and fish have bony skeletons that give them their shape and support.

At birth, a human baby's body has about 300 "soft" bones that will eventually harden and fuse together.

An adult human skeleton has 206 bones that are held together by ligaments.

The spine is made of 26 ring-shaped bones that protect the spinal cord and support the skull.

The skull provides protection for the brain and makes up the structure of the face. The jawbone holds the teeth in place.

The heart, lungs, and liver are all kept safe by the ribs.

Most people have 12 pairs of ribs that are attached in the back to the spine. They are held in place in the front by a strong bone called the sternum.

The longest and strongest bone in the body is the thigh bone, which is called the femur.

A joint is where two bones meet in a skeleton. A hinge joint is like a hinge on a door. Hinge joints allow the arms and legs to bend and straighten at the elbows and knees.

Ball-and-socket joints are found in the shoulders and hips. The round end of one bone fits into a small cup-like area of another bone which allows for movement in every direction.

Bones are made of several layers that include an outer layer that covers the smooth hard part of the bone. It contains nerves and blood vessels that nourish the bone.

Inside the bones is a strong, spongy substance called bone marrow that produces blood cells.

Three Cheers for October PreK–K, SV 9829-9

Accordion Skeleton

Materials

- patterns on pages 34 and 35
- one-inch strips of white copy paper
- black crayon or marker
- scissors
- small thin paper plates
- glue or stapler

Directions

Teacher Preparation: Duplicate the skull, ribs, and hipbone patterns to use as a template.

1. Trace and cut out the skull template on one paper plate. Draw eyes, nose, and mouth.

2. Trace and cut out the ribs and hipbone templates on two additional paper plates.

3. Staple or glue a four-inch strip of paper to the bottom of the skull. Attach the other end of the strip to the top of the ribs to resemble the neck.

4. Staple or glue the bottom of the ribs to the top of the hipbone.

5. Accordion fold four one-inch strips of copy paper for arms and legs. Cut the two arms so that they are shorter than the legs.

6. Staple or glue the arms and legs to the "shoulders" and "hips" as indicated.

7. Hang skeletons from the ceiling or doorway.

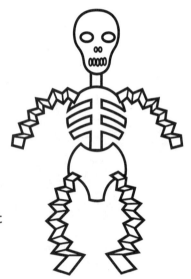

Dog Bone Magnet

Materials

- medium-sized dog milk bones
- white paint
- paintbrushes
- magnetic strip tape
- construction paper
- tiny pom-poms
- wiggly eyes
- scissors
- glue

Directions

1. Paint the dog bone white and allow paint to dry.

2. Glue a strip of magnetic tape on the back of the bone.

3. Glue two wiggly eyes and a pom-pom nose on one end of the bone. Draw a mouth.

4. Cut out rabbit ears from construction paper and glue them on the back of the bone.

5. Use as a refrigerator magnet.

A Bony Snack

You will need

- white bread
- hot dogs cut in half
- toothpicks
- knife
- a round section of a bone from a steak

Directions

1. Trim the crust from a slice of bread.

2. Place the hot dog half on the edge of the bread.

3. Roll the bread around the hot dog and press the edges closed to resemble a bone with the marrow inside. Use a toothpick to hold in place if necessary.

4. Slice the "bone" into thin sections and compare it to the real bone.

5. Enjoy this "bony" snack!

Discuss how the soft spongy part inside a bone is called the bone marrow. Tell children that it produces new blood cells.

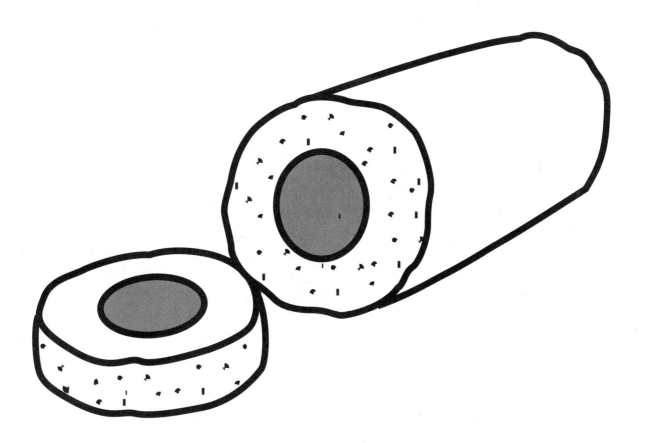

Three Cheers for October PreK–K, SV 9829-9

♫ The Bones in My Body

(Tune: "Skip to My Lou")

In my body, I have a skull.
In my body, I have a skull.
In my body, I have a skull.
My bones make up my skeleton.

In my body, I have some ribs.
In my body, I have some ribs.
In my body, I have some ribs.
My bones make up my skeleton.

In my body, I have arm bones.
In my body, I have arm bones.
In my body, I have arm bones.
My bones make up my skeleton.

In my body, I have leg bones.
In my body, I have leg bones.
In my body, I have leg bones.
My bones make up my skeleton.

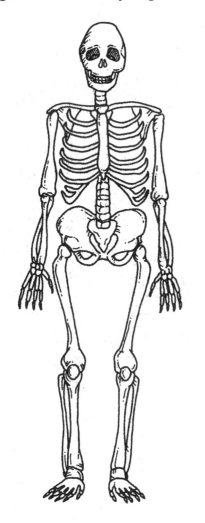

Look Inside These Books About Bones

Boney Bob: The Scared Skeleton
by Keith Faulkner (Little Simon)

Boogie Bones
by Elizabeth Loredo (Putnam Publishing Group)

Dem Bones
by Bob Barner (Chronicle Books)

Funnybones
by Allen Ahlberg (HarperCollins Children's Books)

Rattlebone Rock
by Sylvia Andrews (HarperTrophy)

Skeleton Hiccups
by Margery Cuyler (Margaret K. McElderry)

The Skeleton Inside You
by Philip Balestrino (HarperTrophy)

Three Cheers for October PreK–K, SV 9829-9

Scary Skeletons

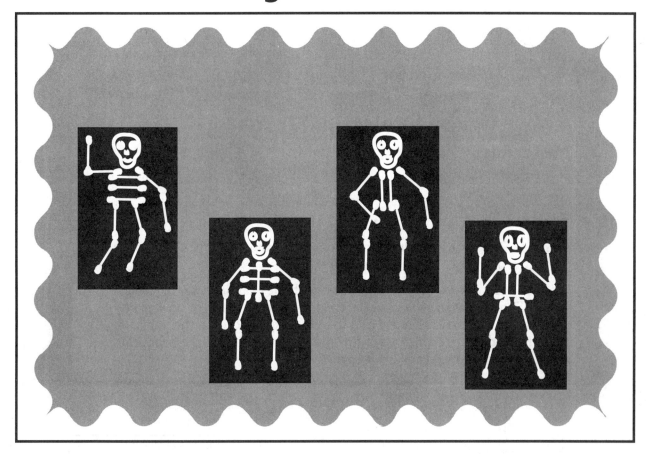

Materials

- white craft paper
- black construction paper
- cotton swabs
- white chalk
- stapler
- border
- glue
- picture of a skeleton

Directions

Teacher Preparation: Cover the board with craft paper.

Discuss the different bones of the skeleton, focusing on the skull, ribs, arms, and legs. The elbows and knees are joints that join two bones and can bend.

1. Draw a skull at the top of the construction paper with the white chalk.

2. Glue cotton swabs to the paper in a skeleton arrangement. Cut cotton swabs in half for the ribs.

Staple the skeletons in a pleasing arrangement on the bulletin board. Add a festive border and caption.

Bony Old Skeletons Centers

Art Center

Science Standard
Understands about scientific inquiry

Skeleton X-rays

Materials

- thin newsprint paper
- glue
- black crayons
- 12" x 12" squares of corrugated cardboard
- clothespins
- 1 or 2 X-rays

Teacher Preparation: Draw the bones of a hand with thick lines of glue on the cardboard. Allow the glue to dry.

Lead a discussion with children about how bones can be seen by using X-rays. Show the real X-rays. Invite children to lay a piece of newsprint paper on top of the cardboard and use clothespins to hold the paper in place. Have them use a black crayon to make a rubbing of the handprint, and it will give the effect of an X-ray.

Block Center

Science Standard
Understands characteristics of organisms

Build a Skeleton

Materials

- pictures of different animal skeletons and a human skeleton
- wooden blocks

Teacher Preparation: Hang skeleton pictures in the block center.

Invite children to copy or to create skeletons using the blocks.

Bony Old Skeletons Centers

 **Dramatic Play Center**

Language Arts Standard
Sequences events accurately

The "Strong Bones" Gym

Materials

- paper towel rolls
- exercise or rest mat
- exercise tape or music
- large wooden block for step aerobics
- medium plastic foam balls
- sweat bands
- clean empty water bottles

Teacher Preparation: Glue a plastic foam ball at each end of the paper towel roll to make a barbell. Fill the bottles with water and have children write their names on their own bottle.

Lead a discussion with children about how exercise makes your bones strong. Invite children to listen to the exercise tape or music and role-play working out at the gym. Have them lie on the mats and do exercises or do step aerobics on the wooden blocks. Encourage children to stop for a drink of water as they exercise.

 **Language Center**

Language Arts Standard
Knows the alphabetical order of letters

Alphabones

Materials

- pattern on page 36
- black marker
- construction paper
- scissors

Teacher Preparation: Duplicate 26 bone patterns on construction paper and cut them out. Write one letter of the alphabet on each pattern.

Invite children to lay the bone cutouts on the table or the floor in alphabetical order.

Bony Old Skeletons Centers

Math Center

Math Standard
Creates a simple graph that uses pictures

Measure Up to the Skeleton

Materials

- cards on page 37
- scissors
- a store-bought paper skeleton that is 3' to 4' tall
- glue
- large piece of craft paper
- index cards

Teacher Preparation: Duplicate and cut out the skeleton cards. Hang the craft paper on the wall and draw three columns, forming a graph. Glue a skeleton card at the top of each column. Hang the paper skeleton on the wall next to the graph, making sure the feet of the skeleton touch the floor.

Invite children to stand next to the skeleton and determine if they are taller than, shorter than, or the same height as the skeleton. Have them write their name on an index card and glue it in the appropriate column of the graph.

Puzzle Center

Science Standard
Understands properties of objects

Pick Up the Pieces

Materials

- pattern on page 36
- scissors
- construction paper
- glue

Teacher Preparation: Duplicate a copy of the skeleton and glue it on construction paper. Enlarge, if desired. Cut it apart into several pieces.

Invite children to put the pieces of the puzzle together to complete the skeleton.

Bony Old Skeletons Centers

Science Center

Bone Detectives

Materials

- collection of animal bones
- magnifying glass
- white play dough
- a toy human skeleton
- pictures of animal skeletons

Invite children to observe the bones using the magnifying glass. Challenge them to reproduce the bone shapes using the play dough.

Writing Center

My Skeleton Book

Materials

- activity masters on pages 38 and 39
- crayons
- construction paper
- pencil
- scissors

Teacher Preparation: Duplicate the activity masters. Make a cover from construction paper and assemble the books. Provide a copy for each child.

Invite children to follow along as you read aloud the sentences on the booklet pages. Have them trace the word and draw the bone that is missing on the skeleton.

Skull and Hipbone Patterns

Use with "Accordion Skeleton" on page 26.

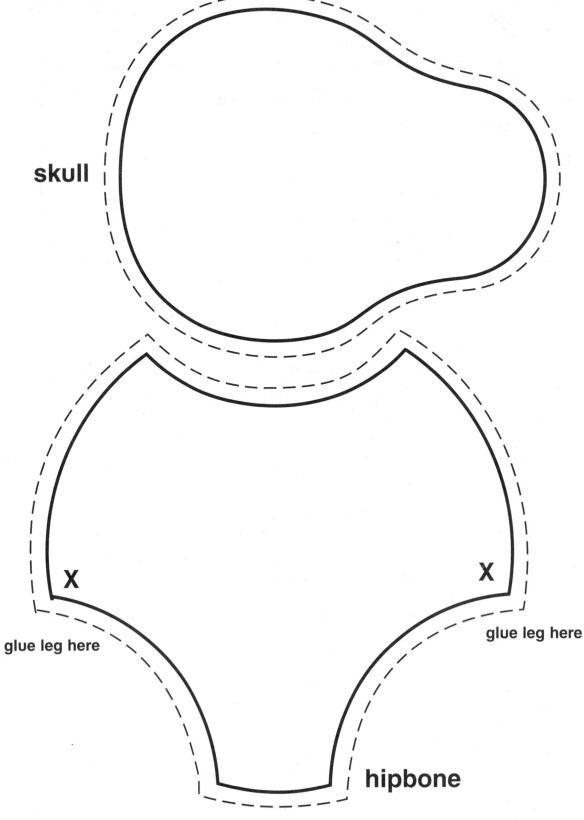

skull

X   X

glue leg here   glue leg here

hipbone

Three Cheers for October PreK–K, SV 9829-9

Ribs Pattern

Use with "Accordion Skeleton" on page 26.

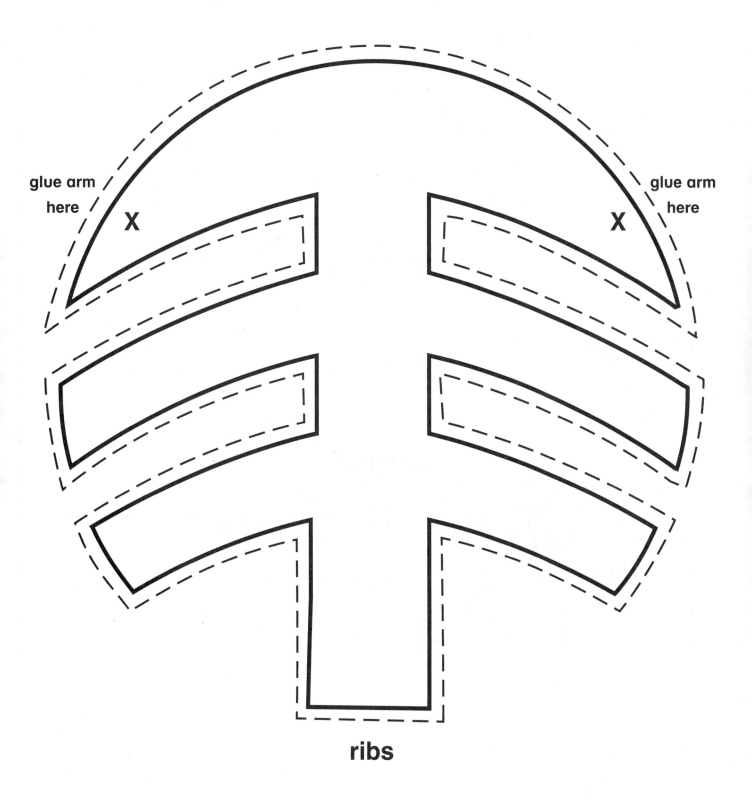

glue arm here X

glue arm here X

ribs

Three Cheers for October PreK–K, SV 9829-9

Bone Pattern

Use with "Alphabones" on page 31.

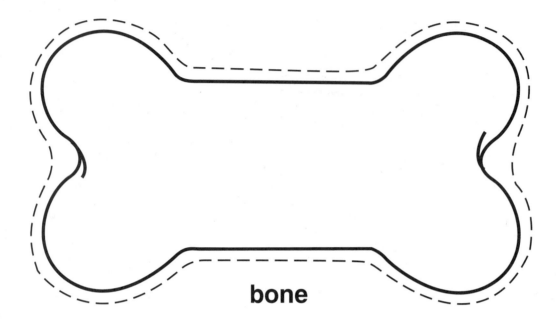

bone

Skeleton Pattern

Use with "Pick Up the Pieces" on page 32.

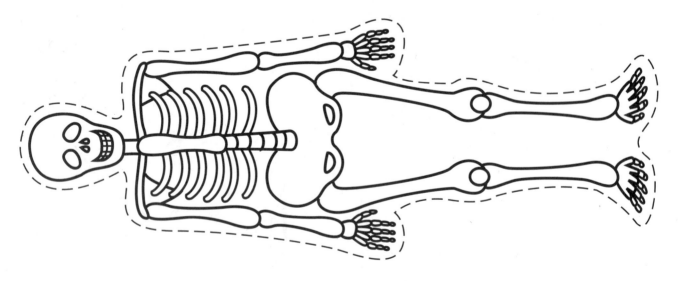

skeleton

Three Cheers for October PreK–K, SV 9829-9

Picture Cards

Use with "Measure Up to the Skeleton" on page 32.

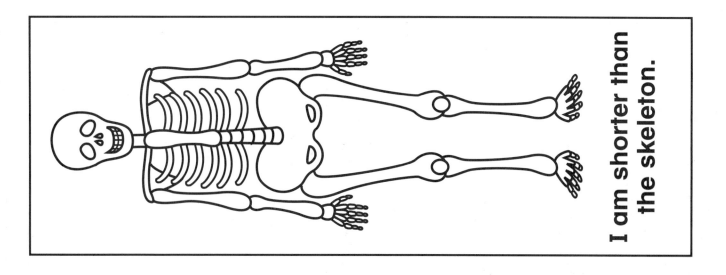

I am shorter than the skeleton.

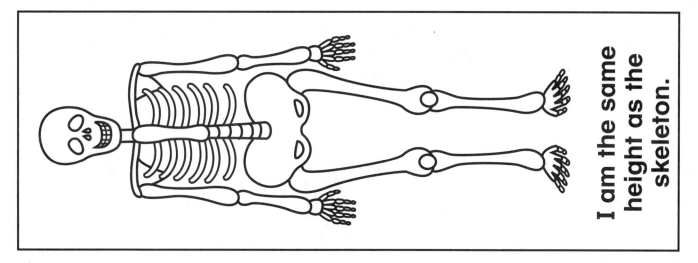

I am the same height as the skeleton.

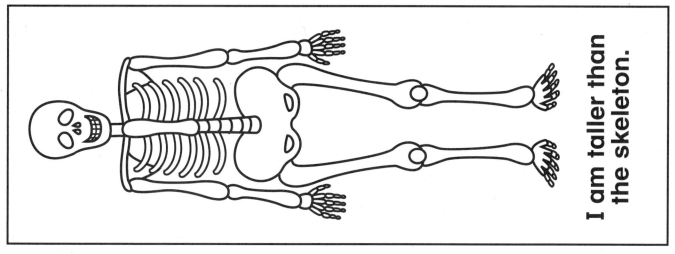

I am taller than the skeleton.

Unit 3, Bony Old Skeletons: Cards
Three Cheers for October PreK–K, SV 9829-9

Skeleton Booklet

Use with "My Skeleton Book" on page 33.

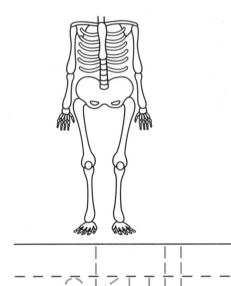

I have a _____ skull _____.

1

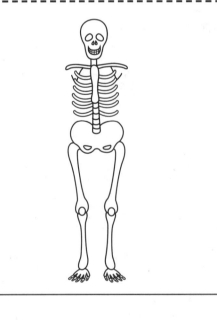

I have _____ arms _____.

2

Unit 3, Bony Old Skeletons: Activity Master
Three Cheers for October PreK–K, SV 9829-9

Skeleton Booklet

Use with "My Skeleton Book" on page 33.

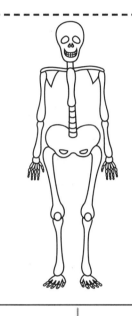

I have _____ ribs _____.

3

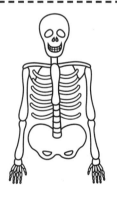

I have _____ legs _____.

4

Unit 3, Bony Old Skeletons: Activity Master
Three Cheers for October PreK–K, SV 9829-9

Spiders Are Spectacular

 Spiders are arachnids, not insects. Spiders have eight legs and two body parts. Insects have six legs and three body parts. Spiders do not have antennae or wings.

 There are over 30,000 species of spiders on all continents of the world except Antarctica.

 A spider has two major body parts, the cephalothorax (the head and chest) and the abdomen.

 Spiders have eight jointed legs that are attached to the cephalothorax. At the end of each leg is a tiny claw that is used for climbing and for manipulating silk.

 Most spiders have eight eyes. Web building spiders have poor eyesight. Hunting spiders have excellent eyesight for short distances.

 Spiders have fangs on each side of their mouth that inject poison and paralyze their prey. Next to the fangs are two pedipalps that help cut and crush their food.

 Spiders have silk spinning glands at the tip of their abdomen called spinnerets. Liquid silk comes from the gland in the abdomen and hardens.

 The silk is used for webs, building traps, wrapping eggs or prey, safety lines, and ballooning.

 Female spiders lay hundreds of eggs and use their silk to make an egg sac to protect the eggs. Most spiders will then abandon the egg sacs. The female wolf spider is one of the only spiders that carries her babies on her back until their first molt (shedding the skin).

 Baby spiders are called spiderlings. Since hundreds of spiderlings hatch at the same time, they must disperse to find places to make their webs and find food. The spiderlings release silk threads and allow the wind to lift them into the air like a balloon and then land in a new area.

Unit 4, Spiders Are Spectacular: Teacher Information
Three Cheers for October PreK–K, SV 9829-9

Silly Spider Hat

Materials

- black construction paper
- sentence strips
- green dot stickers
- stapler
- markers
- scissors
- white crepe paper streamers
- glue

Directions

Teacher Preparation: Cut 1" x 9" strips from the black construction paper. Draw four small *X*'s on each side of the center of a sentence strip to indicate where legs will be attached. Space the marks so that the legs will be above the ears.

1. Accordion fold eight black strips for legs and glue each leg on an indicated mark.

2. Stick two green dots in the center of the sentence strip for large eyes. Use a green marker to draw six smaller dots for the remaining eyes.

3. Staple the sentence strip to form a headband. Adjust the band to fit.

4. Cut several two-foot lengths of white crepe paper and staple to the back of the headband to resemble silk threads.

The Itsy Bitsy Spider

Materials

- pattern on page 49
- manila paper
- markers
- scissors
- glue
- bendable straws
- spider rings
- tape

Directions

Teacher Preparation: Duplicate a copy of the house for each child.

1. Color and cut out the house. Glue it on manila paper.

2. Draw grass, sun, and trees with markers.

3. Turn a straw upside down and bend it to resemble a waterspout.

4. Slip the straw through the spider ring and tape the straw to the side of the house. Place tape at the top and bottom of the straw so that the spider can slide up and down the "waterspout."

5. Sing "The Itsy Bitsy Spider" and move the spider up and down the spout.

Scrumptious Spiders

You will need

- crème-filled cookies
- Chinese noodles
- small tube of colored frosting
- paper plates
- crayons or markers

Directions

1. Start with two cookies and eight Chinese noodles.

2. Stick eight noodles into the crème part of one cookie with four on each side.

3. Lay the cookie with the noodle legs next to a second cookie to form the two parts of the spider's body.

4. Use the tube of frosting to make eight eyes on the spider.

5. Draw a spider web on the paper plate using the tube frosting. Place the cookie spider in the middle of the web.

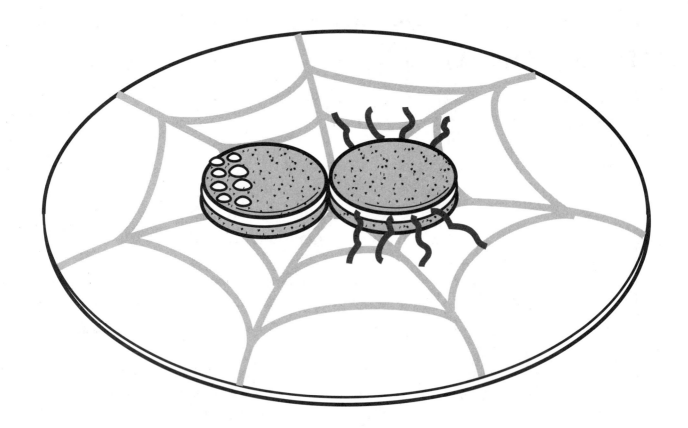

Three Cheers for October PreK–K, SV 9829-9

Little Miss Muffet

Little Miss Muffet sat on a tuffet,

  (Sweep arms from side to side and say, "Tra la tra la tra la.")

Eating her curds and whey.

  (Slap thighs twice, rub tummy, say, "Mmmm." Repeat three times.)

Along came a spider and sat down beside her,

  (Say, "Dum de dum dum dummmmm," in a mysterious tone.)

And frightened Miss Muffet away.

  (Move arms in a sweeping motion and say, "Swoosh!")

Special Spider Stories

Be Nice to Spiders
by Margaret Bloy Graham (HarperCollins)

The Itsy Bitsy Spider
by Iza Trapini (Charlesbridge Publishing)

Miss Spider's Tea Party
by David Kirk (Scholastic)

Spectacular Spiders
by Linda Glaser (Millbrook Press)

Spiders
by Gail Gibbons (Holiday House)

Spider's Lunch
by Joanna Cole (Grosset & Dunlap)

Spiders Spin Webs
by Yvonne Winer (Charlesbridge Publishing)

The Very Busy Spider
by Eric Carle (Scholastic)

Special Spiders

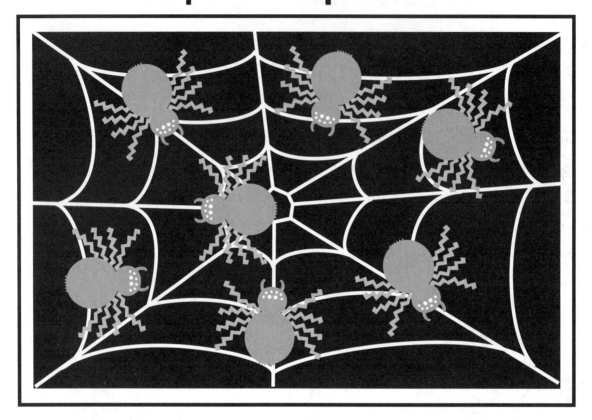

Materials

- pattern on page 50
- black craft paper
- orange construction paper
- white chalk
- a fine-tip black marker
- border
- scissors
- glue

Directions

Teacher Preparation: Duplicate a copy of the spider to use as a template. Cut 1" x 6" strips from the orange paper. Cover the bulletin board with black craft paper and draw a large orb web with white chalk. For younger children, draw small dots on the spider body to indicate where to glue the legs.

Read one of the spider books from the list on page 43 and introduce children to the actual names and functions of the body parts of a spider.

1. Trace and cut out the spider body on the orange construction paper.

2. Accordion fold eight paper strips for the legs.

3. Glue four legs on each side of the spider. Overlap the strips to fit.

4. Use a black marker to draw eight eyes on the spider.

5. Arrange and staple the spiders on the board in a pleasing arrangement.

6. Add a festive border and the caption.

Three Cheers for October PreK–K, SV 9829-9

Spiders Are Spectacular Centers

Art Center

Science Standard
Understands properties of materials

Spider Web Art

Materials

- an empty shoe box
- black construction paper
- a spoon
- clear tape
- white tempera paint in a bowl
- several marbles
- plastic spider rings

Teacher Preparation: Cut construction paper to fit the bottom of the shoe box. Drop the marbles in the white paint.

Invite children to lay a piece of black paper in the bottom of the box. Then have them pick up the marbles with the spoon and drop them into the box. Have children put the lid on the box and shake it so the marbles roll around inside. Remove the paper, allow it to dry, and tape a spider ring on the "web."

Game Center

Social Studies Standard
Follows rules such as taking turns

Beanbag Toss

Materials

- large piece of craft paper
- masking tape
- 20–30 spider rings
- black marker
- a beanbag

Teacher Preparation: Draw a large spider web on the craft paper, leaving wide spaces between the lines of the web. In random order, write a number from 0–3 in each section of the web. Repeat numbers as often as needed. Tape the paper to the floor.

Invite children to stand several feet from the "web" and toss the beanbag. Have them name the number on which it lands. Then have them place the corresponding number of spider rings on their fingers. Have them continue taking turns until their hands are full of rings.

Spiders Are Spectacular Centers

Language Center

Language Arts Standard
Recognizes uppercase and lowercase letters

Can You Spell *Spider*?

Materials

- patterns on page 51
- crayons
- sharp-tip marker
- file folder
- scissors
- blank die
- 12 plastic tokens
- glue

Teacher Preparation: Duplicate two copies of the patterns. Color and cut out the spider webs and the boxes. Then glue them to the inside of the file folder, making two game boards. Write one lowercase letter from the word *spider* on each side of the blank die.

Invite children to take turns rolling the die to spell *spider*. Have children cover the letter on the file folder with a plastic token for each letter that is rolled. For older children, have them cover the letters in sequence rather than at random.

Math Center

Math Standard
Distinguishes between odd and even numbers

Spiders on the Waterspout

Materials

- patterns on page 52
- glue
- two plastic spiders that are different colors
- file folder
- scissors
- sharp-tip marker
- markers
- blank die

Teacher Preparation: Duplicate, color, and cut out the patterns. Glue the waterspout on the inside of a file folder, with the puddle at the bottom and the sun at the top. Write a number from 1–4 on four sides of the blank die. Draw a raindrop on two sides of the die.

Introduce odd and even numbers to children. Invite children to take turns rolling the die to move their spider up the waterspout. Challenge children to tell if the number rolled is odd or even. If the raindrop is rolled, the spider is "washed out" and has to start over again.

Spiders Are Spectacular Centers

Music Center

Language Arts Standard
Understands how reading works from left to right

Itsy Bitsy Tunes

Materials

- xylophone with colored keys
- chart paper
- markers

Teacher Preparation: Prepare a chart that shows the musical notes of "The Itsy Bitsy Spider." Color code the notes to match the keys on the xylophone. Hang the chart in the music center.

Invite children to play the song according to the colors of the notes on the chart and the keys on the xylophone. Have them follow the notes from left to right.

Reading Center

Language Arts Standard
Sequences events accurately

Sequencing the Rhyme

Materials

- cards on page 53
- crayons or markers
- construction paper
- glue

Teacher Preparation: Duplicate, color, and cut out the cards. Glue them on construction paper.

Invite children to say the nursery rhyme "Little Miss Muffet" and put the pictures in the correct sequence.

Spiders Are Spectacular Centers

Science Center

Science Standard
Understands about scientific inquiry

Take a Good Look

Materials

- nonfiction spider books
- drawing paper
- toy spiders
- crayons

Discuss with children the two parts of a spider's body, the eight legs, and multiple eyes (most spiders have eight eyes). Invite them to draw a picture of a spider by looking at the toy spiders or at a picture in a book.

Writing Center

Math Standard
Knows spatial relationships

See the Spider Go

Materials

- activity masters on pages 54 and 55
- construction paper
- scissors
- crayons or markers
- stapler
- pencils

Teacher Preparation: Duplicate and cut apart the booklet masters. Make covers from construction paper and assemble the books. Provide a copy for each child.

Read the booklet to children and have them follow along. Then invite them to trace the position word and draw the spider to match the sentence.

House Pattern

Use with "The Itsy Bitsy Spider" on page 41.

house

Unit 4, Spiders Are Spectacular: Pattern
Three Cheers for October PreK–K, SV 9829-9

Spider Pattern

Use with "Special Spiders" on page 44.

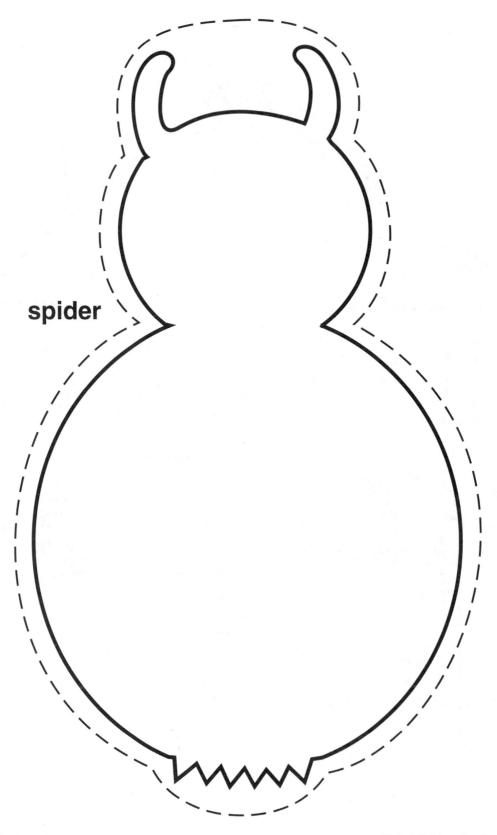

spider

Three Cheers for October PreK–K, SV 9829-9

Spider Game Patterns

Use with "Can You Spell *Spider?*" on page 46.

S

P

I

D

E

R

Waterspout Game Patterns

Use with "Spiders on the Waterspout" on page 46.

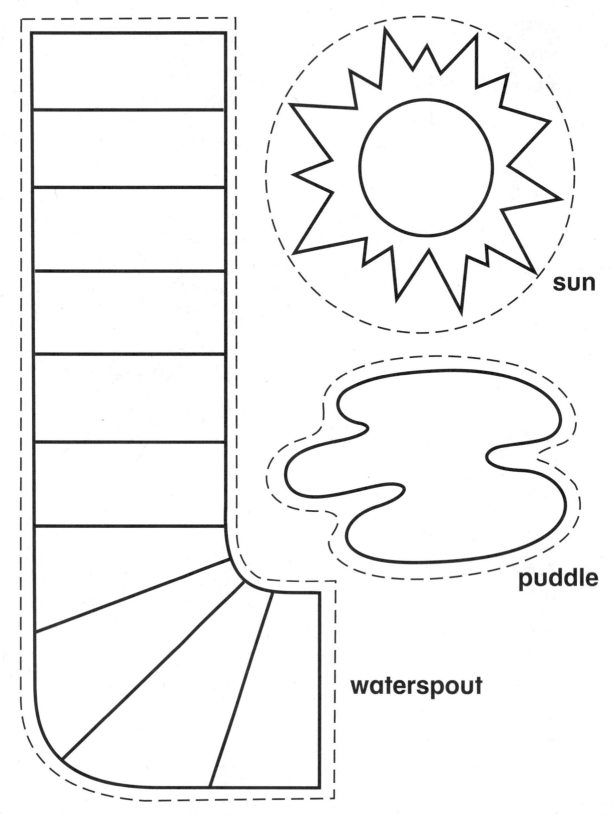

sun

puddle

waterspout

Three Cheers for October PreK–K, SV 9829-9

Sequence Cards

Use with "Sequencing the Rhyme" on page 47.

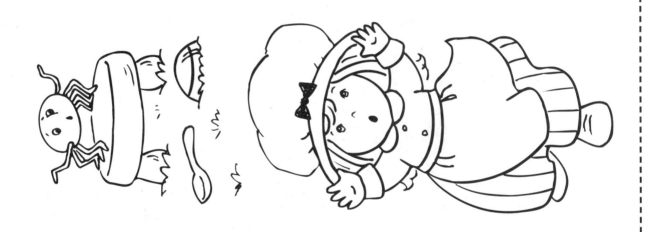

53

Position Booklet

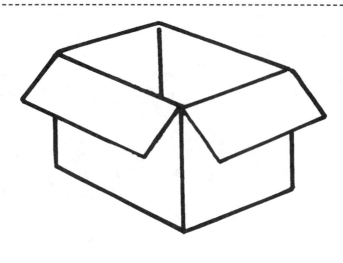

The spider is _____in_____ the box.

1

The spider is _____on_____ the bed.

2

Directions: Use with "See the Spider Go" on page 48. Read the booklet to children and have them follow along. Then invite them to trace the position word and draw the spider to match the sentence.

Three Cheers for October PreK–K, SV 9829-9

Position Booklet

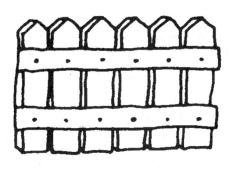

The spider is ___above___ the fence.

3

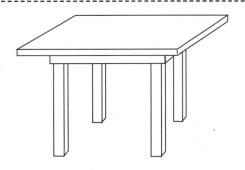

The spider is ___under___ the table.

4

Directions: Use with "See the Spider Go" on page 48. Read the booklet to children and have them follow along. Then invite them to trace the position word and draw the spider to match the sentence.

www.harcourtschoolsupply.com

55

Unit 4, Spiders Are Spectacular: Activity Master

Three Cheers for October PreK–K, SV 9829-9

When Fall Comes

 The fall season officially begins in the Northern Hemisphere on September 22, the Autumn Equinox.

 The Autumn Equinox is when there are twelve hours of daylight and twelve hours of night.

 Gradually the days will get shorter and the nights will get longer. The temperatures also begin to get cooler.

 These are nature's signs to plant and animal life to begin to prepare for winter. Winter will bring colder temperatures and little or no food.

 Plants and trees make their own food by turning carbon dioxide and water into food. They need sunlight and chlorophyll for this. Chlorophyll is what makes the leaves green.

Many plants and trees stop making food in the fall to prepare for winter. The chlorophyll then fades away, and the red, orange, and yellow colors are seen. These colors have been there all summer, but the green chlorophyll covered them up.

 The leaves then fall off, and the plants and trees begin to make a corklike substance to seal the area where the leaves were attached. This protects the plant or tree from the cold temperatures of winter. They lie dormant during the winter months.

 Since food sources and temperatures change during the winter, animals survive by hibernating, migrating, or adapting.

 Some animals, like geese, butterflies, and bats, migrate to warmer places to find food. These animals may travel a thousand miles or more.

 Other animals prepare for winter during autumn by gathering and storing or eating large quantities of food.

 Animals that hibernate eat large quantities of food in preparation for the winter months. Grizzly bears can gain up to 40 pounds in one week.

Squirrel in a Tree

Materials

- pattern on page 65
- empty paper towel tubes
- brown tempera paint
- tissue paper the color of fall leaves
- paintbrushes
- scissors
- crayons
- glue

Directions

Teacher Preparation: Duplicate a copy of the squirrel pattern for each child. Cut tissue paper into one-inch squares. Cut a hole in the side of each paper towel tube to resemble a hole in the side of a tree.

1. Paint the paper towel tube brown and allow it to dry.

2. Make several three-inch cuts on one end of the paper towel tube. Bend the sections outward to resemble the branches of a tree.

3. Crumple a generous amount of tissue paper squares and glue them on the "branches" of the tree.

4. Color and cut out the squirrel pattern.

5. Insert the squirrel in the tree hole. Glue it in place so that it appears to be in the tree.

Note: This can be used in the math center on page 62.

Leaf Prints

Materials

- various types of leaves that are still pliable
- construction paper
- tempera paint
- paintbrushes
- small towel

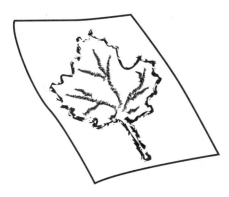

Directions

1. Place the towel under the construction paper.

2. Paint the underside of a leaf where the veins are most visible.

3. Lay the leaf on the construction paper with the painted side down.

4. Cover the leaf with a second piece of paper and rub firmly over the leaf with the palm of your hand.

5. Remove the paper covering the leaf and the leaf to see the leaf print.

Magic Tree Cookies

You will need

- poem on page 65
- leaf cookie cutter
- sugar cookie dough
- white cake frosting
- red, green, yellow food coloring
- resealable plastic bag
- plastic knives
- paper napkins
- three empty butter tubs with lids
- a small tote bag

Directions

Teacher Preparation: Roll out cookie dough and cut a cookie for each child with the leaf cookie cutter. Bake according to directions and cool. Place cookies in a resealable bag. Divide frosting into the three butter tubs. Add a few drops of food coloring to each one and stir until thoroughly mixed.

1. Place the cookies, butter tubs, knives, napkins, and the poem in the tote bag. Then find a tree whose leaves are beginning to change colors and hang the bag on one of the branches.

2. Discuss with children how the leaves on trees seem to "magically" change colors.

3. Go on a nature walk to observe the leaves and discover the bag of cookies. Read the "Magic Tree Poem" to the children.

4. Have children choose their favorite color of icing and frost their cookie.

Extension: Add the materials for "A 'Hand'-some Tree" on page 61 to the tote bag. Have children paint the magic tree after they eat their cookie.

Three Cheers for October PreK–K, SV 9829-9

🎵 Fall Is Here

(Tune: "London Bridge")

See the leaves all falling down,
 falling down, falling down.
See the leaves all falling down. Fall is here.

Feel the weather getting cool,
 getting cool, getting cool.
Feel the weather getting cool. Fall is here.

See the squirrels gather nuts, gather nuts, gather nuts.
See the squirrels gather nuts. Fall is here.

Hear the geese as they fly south, they fly south, they fly south.
Hear the geese as they fly south. Fall is here.

Fall into These Stories

Autumn Leaves
by Ken Robbins (Scholastic)

How Do You Know It's Fall?
by Allan Fowler (Children's Press)

It's Fall
by Linda Glaser (Millbrook Press)

Nuts to You
by Lois Ehlert (Harcourt Children's Books)

Red Leaf, Yellow Leaf
by Lois Ehlert (Harcourt Children's Books)

When Autumn Comes
by Robert Maass (Henry Holt & Company)

Why Do Leaves Change Colors?
by Betsy Maestro (HarperTrophy)

Fall Is All Around

Materials

- pattern on page 66
- scissors
- stapler
- craft paper
- white construction paper
- tempera paint in fall colors
- paintbrushes
- sponges
- border

Directions

Teacher Preparation: Duplicate the leaf pattern on construction paper. Provide a copy for each child. Cover bulletin board with craft paper. Draw or paint a large tree in the center of the bulletin board.

1. Cut out the leaf pattern.

2. Use a sponge to paint the leaf.

Arrange and staple the leaves in a pleasing arrangement on the bulletin board. Add a festive border and the caption.

When Fall Comes Centers

Art Center

Science Standard
Understands properties of materials

A "Hand"-some Tree

Materials

- white construction paper
- leaf confetti
- glue
- watercolor paints
- crayons

Have children use a crayon to trace around their hand and wrist on the construction paper so that it resembles a tree trunk and branches. Then have them color the "tree." Invite them to use fall colors to paint small leaves on the branches of the tree with the watercolors. Have children glue several confetti leaves on the tree to add some sparkle. Use this with the "Magic Tree Cookies" on page 58.

Game Center

Math Standard
Applies and adapts a variety of strategies to solve problems

An A-MAZE-ing Squirrel

Materials

- pattern on page 67
- glue
- washable markers
- spray bottle filled with water
- construction paper
- markers
- scissors
- paper towels

Teacher Preparation: Duplicate and color the maze pattern. Glue the maze on construction paper and laminate.

Have children use washable markers to help the squirrel find the acorns. Encourage children to wipe the game board when they are finished.

When Fall Comes Centers

Language Center

Language Arts Standard
Knows the alphabetical order of the letters of the alphabet

Alphabetical Leaves

Materials

- patterns on page 68
- construction paper in fall colors
- black marker
- scissors

Teacher Preparation: Duplicate 26 leaves on construction paper and write one letter of the alphabet on each leaf. Cut them out and laminate them for durability.

Invite children to lay the leaves on the table or floor in alphabetical order.

Math Center

Math Standard
Associates numerals with sets of objects

Feed the Squirrel

Materials

- craft made in "Squirrel in a Tree" on page 57
- 6–12 acorns
- resealable plastic bag
- dice

Teacher Preparation: Collect acorns or, if possible, have children go on a nature walk to collect them. Provide each child with one die and six acorns or two dice and twelve acorns in a resealable plastic bag.

Have children stand their "tree" on a flat surface. Then have them roll the die or dice. Have children drop the corresponding number of acorns in the tree for the squirrel. Have them lift the tree to remove the acorns and roll again.

When Fall Comes Centers

Reading Center

Language Arts Standard
Reads simple high-frequency words

Fall Colors

Materials

- cards on page 69
- markers
- magnetic letters
- magnetic board
- scissors
- magnetic tape

Teacher Preparation: Duplicate and cut out the cards. Color the leaves according to the color word on each card. Stick a piece of magnetic tape on the back of each picture card.

Invite children to use the magnetic letters on the board to spell the color words on each picture card.

Science Center

Science Standard
Collects data gained from direct experience

Observing Pine Cones

Materials

- pine cones of different sizes
- magnifying glass
- bowl of water

Invite children to use the magnifying glass to observe the open pine cone scales. Then have them place one pine cone in the bowl of water. Leave the pine cone in the water for about two hours. Have children observe the pine cone again with the magnifying glass. The pine cone will be closed. Encourage children to describe the changes that they have seen. Also, have them predict if the pine cone will open up again if left out of the water.

When Fall Comes Centers

Sensory Center

Math Standard
Sorts by size, color, shape, or kind

"Nuts" for You

Materials

- plastic tub
- fall leaves
- pecans, acorns, walnuts, or other nuts

Teacher Preparation: Place the nuts in the tub and cover them with the leaves.

Invite children to find the nuts and sort them by size, kind, or texture.

Note: Be aware of children with food allergies.

Writing Center

Language Arts Standard
Makes illustrations to match sentences

I Like Fall

Materials

- activity master on page 70
- white construction paper
- pencils
- crayons

Teacher Preparation: Duplicate the activity master on construction paper.

Invite children to draw and color a picture of their favorite thing about fall. Then have them write or dictate an answer to complete the sentence.

Squirrel Pattern

Use with "Squirrel in a Tree" on page 57.

squirrel

Magic Tree Poem

Use with "Magic Tree Cookies" on page 58.

Here are some leaf cookies from my tree.

Enjoy them and draw a nice picture of me.

Love,

The Magic Tree

Leaf Pattern

Use with "Fall Is All Around" on page 60.

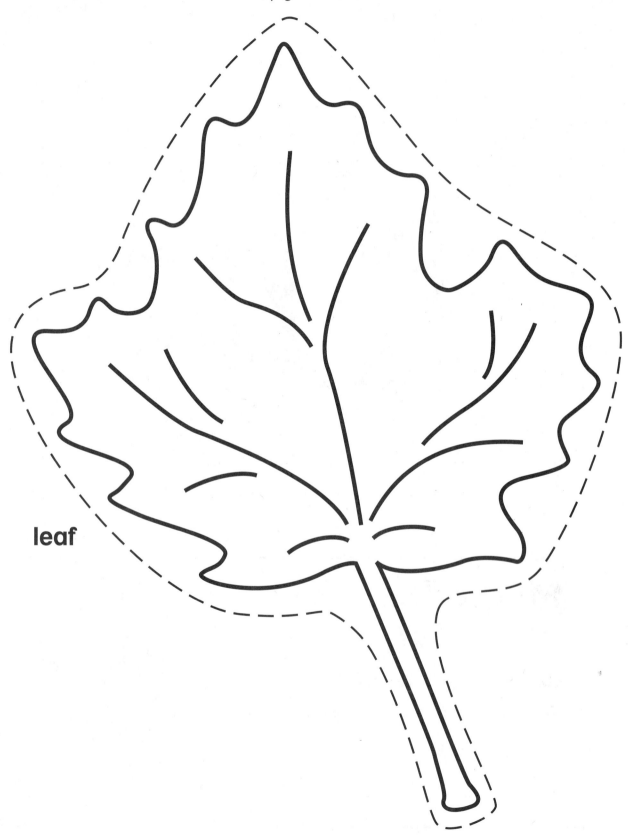

leaf

Three Cheers for October PreK–K, SV 9829-9

Squirrel Maze Pattern

Use with "An A-MAZE-ing Squirrel" on page 61.

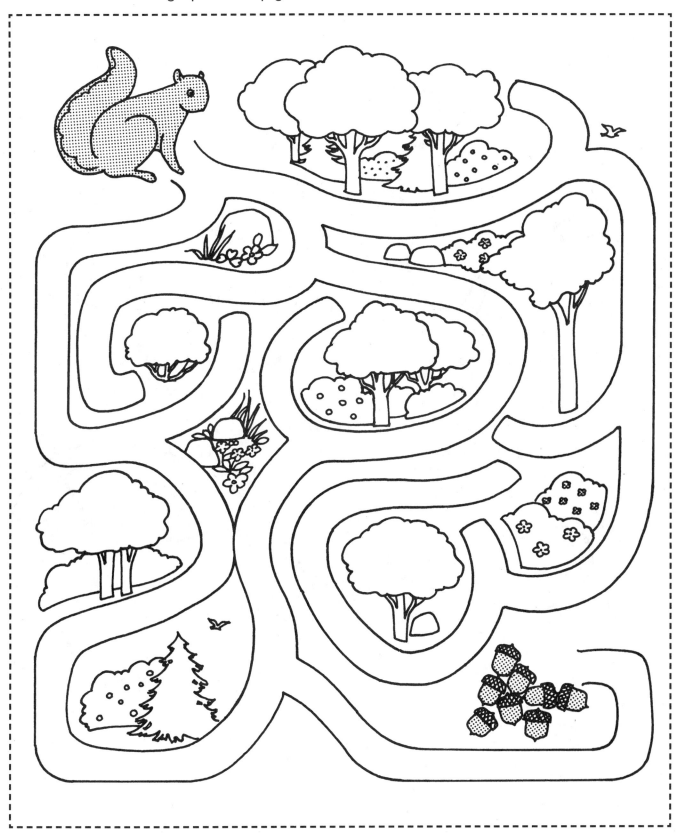

Unit 5, When Fall Comes: Pattern
Three Cheers for October PreK–K, SV 9829-9

Alphabet Leaf Patterns
Use with "Alphabetical Leaves" on page 62.

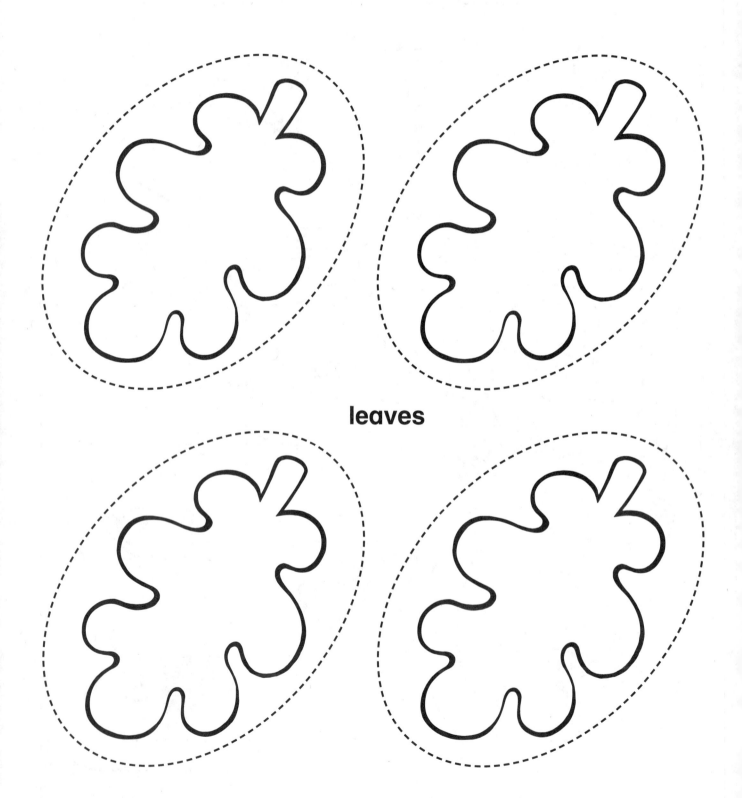

leaves

Word Cards

Use with "Fall Colors" on page 63.

a **red** leaf

a **brown** leaf

a **yellow** leaf

an **orange** leaf

Unit 5, When Fall Comes: Cards
Three Cheers for October PreK–K, SV 9829-9

Name _____

Fall

My favorite thing about fall is

_____

- -

_____

_____

- -

because _____

_____

- -

_____.

Directions: Use with "I Like Fall" on page 64. Invite children to draw and color a picture of their favorite thing about fall. Then have them write or dictate an answer to complete the sentence.

70

It's Pumpkin Pickin' Time

 Pumpkins are believed to have originated in Central America as far back as 6000 B.C.

 The name *pumpkin* comes from the Greek word *pepon*, which means "large melon."

 A pumpkin is a fruit that is 90 percent water and contains potassium and Vitamin A.

 Pumpkins range in size from less than a pound to over 1,000 pounds.

 A leafy vine grows from a pumpkin seed, and yellowish orange flowers bloom on the vine.

 If pollination occurs, the ovaries at the base of the flower will swell and become tiny green pumpkins. The pumpkins continue to grow larger and begin to change color. About four months after planting, they are ready to harvest.

 Pumpkins can vary in color from white to yellow to orange. The orange Connecticut field variety is the traditional American pumpkin.

 Native Americans used pumpkins for food and also used flattened strips of dried pumpkins to make mats.

 Colonists sliced off pumpkin tips and removed the seeds. They then filled the insides with milk, spices, and honey. This was baked in hot ashes and is the origin of pumpkin pie.

 When the Irish immigrated to America, they brought with them the tradition of carving turnips at Halloween. However, they found that pumpkins were plentiful and much easier to carve.

Inside and Outside

Materials

- pattern on page 81
- pumpkin
- knife

- orange, yellow, and green construction paper
- yellow yarn

- scissors
- glue
- crayons

Directions

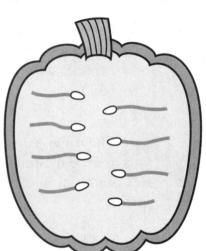

Teacher Preparation: Duplicate a copy of the pumpkin pattern on both the orange and the yellow construction paper for each child.

Have children describe the outside of the pumpkin. Then cut the top off of the pumpkin so they can observe the pulp, the strings, and the seeds.

1. Cut out the orange and yellow pumpkins and glue them together.

2. Draw and cut out a stem from a small piece of green construction paper. Glue it to the top of the pumpkin.

3. Draw vertical lines on the orange pumpkin with a dark crayon to resemble the outside of the pumpkin.

4. Cut yarn into three-inch sections. Glue several pieces on the yellow pumpkin to resemble the inside.

5. Rinse and dry several seeds from the pumpkin. Then glue one seed at the end of each piece of yarn to complete the pumpkin.

Pumpkin Mask

Materials

- patterns on page 80
- 9-inch paper plates
- orange tempera paint

- paintbrushes
- green construction paper
- scissors

- elastic cord
- orange pony beads
- hole punch

Directions

Teacher Preparation: Cut out the mask pattern to use as a template. Trace the template on a paper plate. Cut out the mask and the eye holes. Duplicate the stem and vine patterns on green construction paper.

1. Paint the mask orange and allow it to dry.

2. Cut out the stem and vine. Glue them to the top of the mask.

3. Punch a hole on each side of the mask.

4. Thread each end of the elastic cord through a punched hole in the mask and through one bead. Tie a knot to secure.

A Tasty, Toasty Jack-o'-lantern

You will need

- a half of an English muffin per child
- apricot jelly or jam
- raisins
- celery
- toaster
- plastic knives
- napkins

Directions

Teacher Preparation: Cut celery into one-inch pieces.

1. Toast the English muffins.
2. Spread apricot jelly or jam on the muffin for orange color.
3. Make eyes, nose, and mouth with raisins.
4. Add a small piece of celery for the stem.
5. Enjoy this tasty, toasty snack!

Three Cheers for October PreK–K, SV 9829-9

Five Little Pumpkins Finger Play

Five little pumpkins sitting on a gate. (five fingers up)

The first one said, "Oh my, it's getting late." (hands on cheeks)

The second one said, "There's a chill in the air." (arms around self)

The third one said, "But we don't care." (swing pointer finger)

The fourth one said, "We're ready for some fun!" (hands in cheering motion)

The fifth one said, "Let's run and run and run." (running motion)

So w-o-o-o-o-o went the wind and out went the lights. (clap)

And the five little pumpkins rolled out of sight! (arms in rolling motion)

Pick a Good One from This Patch of Books

I Like Pumpkins
by Jerry Smath (Cartwheel Books)

It's Pumpkin Time
by Zoe Hall (Scholastic)

The Little Old Lady Who Was Not Afraid of Anything
by Linda Williams (HarperTrophy)

Patty's Pumpkin Patch
by Teri Sloat (Putnam Publishing Group)

Pumpkin Day, Pumpkin Night
by Anne Rockwell (Walker & Company)

Pumpkin, Pumpkin
by Jeanne Titherington (HarperTrophy)

Too Many Pumpkins
by Linda White (Holiday House)

The Pumpkin Book
by Gail Gibbons (Holiday House)

Three Cheers for October PreK–K, SV 9829-9

It's Pumpkin Pickin' Time

Materials

- blue, green, and brown craft paper
- pattern on page 81
- scissors
- border
- white and green construction paper
- glue
- newspaper
- stapler
- orange tempera paint
- paintbrushes
- crayons or markers

Directions

Teacher Preparation: Cover the top half of the bulletin board with blue craft paper and the bottom half with brown. Cut the green craft paper into sections that are one foot wide and several feet long. Twist these pieces to resemble pumpkin vines and staple in a random order on the bulletin board. Cut green leaves and staple them to the vines. Duplicate two pumpkin patterns on white construction paper per child. Add a festive border and caption.

1. Cut out two pumpkins and paint them orange.

2. Draw and cut out a stem. Glue it to the top of the pumpkin.

3. Staple the two pumpkin shapes together, leaving the bottom edge open.

4. Stuff the pumpkin with newspaper and staple the bottom edge closed.

5. Arrange and staple pumpkins to the vines on the bulletin board.

Three Cheers for October PreK–K, SV 9829-9

It's Pumpkin Pickin' Time Centers

Art Center

Soda Bottle Jack-o'-lanterns

Materials

- patterns on page 82
- empty 2-liter soda bottles
- funnel
- orange and green tempera paint
- scissors
- yellow construction paper
- glue
- paintbrushes
- water

Teacher Preparation: Duplicate patterns on yellow construction paper for each child. Mix orange paint with a small amount of water to thin the paint.

Have children pour about a half cup of orange paint into a soda bottle using the funnel. Then have them tighten the bottle lid, shake the bottle until it is thoroughly coated with paint, and pour out any remaining paint. Have children replace the lid and then paint it green. Invite children to cut out eyes, a nose, and a mouth and glue them to the outside of the bottle for the face of the jack-o'-lantern.

Tip: These bottles can be used in the block center activity on page 77.

Language Center

My Fat Pumpkin

Materials

- activity master on page 83
- crayons
- pencil

Teacher Preparation: Duplicate a copy of the activity master for each child.

Invite children to read each word using onset/rime patterns. Have them color each section of the pumpkin orange and the stem green after they read the word. Have them color the blank sections blue.

It's Pumpkin Pickin' Time Centers

Block Center

Social Studies Standard
Follows rules such as taking turns

Bottle Bowling

Materials

- bottles made in "Soda Bottle Jack-o'-lanterns" on page 76
- a rubber ball
- wooden blocks

Invite children to set up several soda bottles like bowling pins. Then have them use the wooden blocks to make the sides of the bowling lane. Encourage them to take turns rolling the ball to knock down the bottles.

Math Center

Math Standard
Associates numerals up to 10 with sets of objects

How Many Seeds?

Materials

- medium pumpkin
- newspaper
- two- or three-foot piece of craft paper
- knife
- colander
- marker

Teacher Preparation: Cut the top off of the pumpkin and remove the seeds. Place them in the colander and rinse. You may wish to use the seeds from the science center activity on page 79.

Have children estimate how many seeds they think are in the pumpkin. Record their guesses on the chalkboard. Lay the craft paper on the floor. Invite children to count ten seeds. Lay each set of ten on the craft paper and circle each set with the marker. Challenge older children to count by 10's to find the total number of seeds. Check children's guesses to see whose was the closest.

It's Pumpkin Pickin' Time Centers

Reading Center

Language Arts Standard
Sequences events accurately

From Seed to Pumpkin

Materials

- cards on page 84
- crayons or markers
- construction paper
- glue
- a book selection that includes the life cycle of the pumpkin plant

Teacher Preparation: Duplicate, color, and cut out the picture cards. Glue them on construction paper.

Read aloud the book selection and discuss with children how a pumpkin grows. Invite them to put the picture cards in the correct sequence.

Sensory Center

Science Standard
Understands properties of materials

Pumpkin Pie Play Dough

Materials

- 5½ cups flour
- 8 teaspoons cream of tartar
- orange food coloring
- 4 cups water
- pumpkin cookie cutters
- 2 cups salt
- ¾ cup oil
- 1½ ounces of pumpkin pie spice
- medium saucepan

Teacher Preparation: Mix all of the ingredients together. Cook and stir over medium heat until dough forms. Cool and knead the dough until smooth.

Have children flatten the play dough and use the cookie cutters to make pumpkins.

It's Pumpkin Pickin' Time Centers

Science Center

Science Standard
Collects data from direct experience

Out Come the Seeds

Materials

- medium pumpkin
- newspaper
- knife
- colander

Teacher Preparation: Cut the top off of the pumpkin. Set the pumpkin on newspapers on the science table.

Invite children to use their hands to pull the seeds out of the pumpkin. Have them collect the seeds in the colander. Have children place the colander in the sink and rinse the seeds. Save the seeds to use with the math center activity on page 77.

Writing Center

Language Arts Standard
Uses descriptive vocabulary

The Pumpkin Is . . .

Materials

- activity master on page 85
- pencil
- pumpkin
- crayons

Teacher Preparation: Duplicate a copy of the activity master for each child.

Have children look at the size, shape, color, and texture of the pumpkin. Have them write or dictate a word that describes the pumpkin to complete the sentence. Invite them to draw a picture of the pumpkin.

Pumpkin Mask Patterns

Use with "Pumpkin Mask" on page 72.

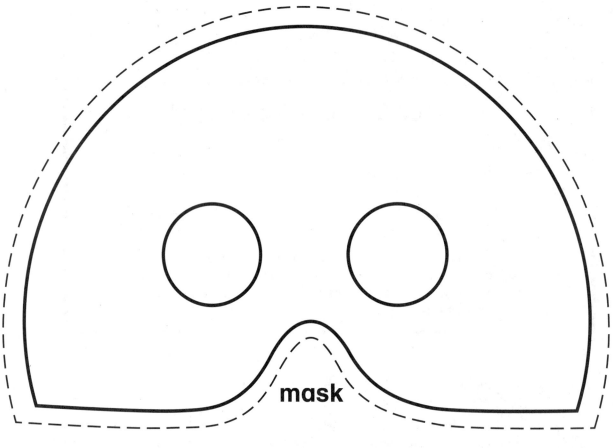

mask

stem

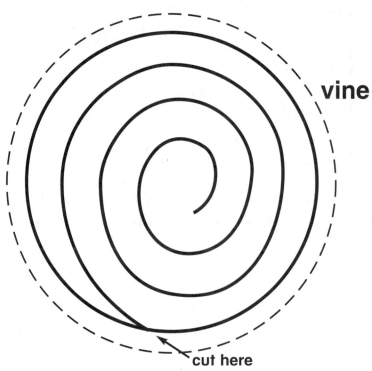

vine

cut here

Unit 6, It's Pumpkin Pickin' Time: Patterns
Three Cheers for October PreK–K, SV 9829-9

Pumpkin Pattern

Use with "Inside and Outside" on page 72 and "It's Pumpkin Pickin' Time" on page 75.

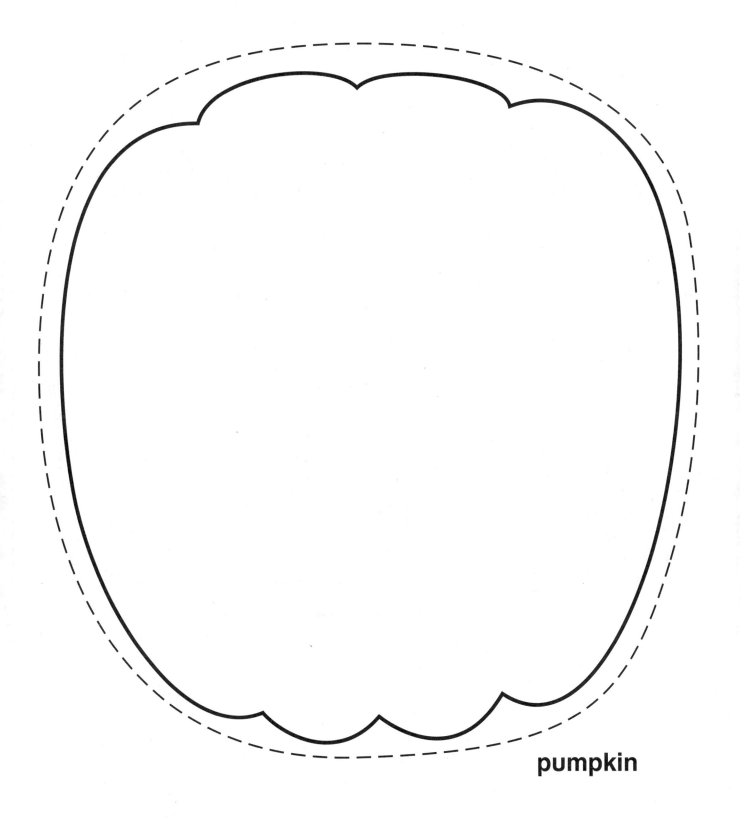

pumpkin

Face Patterns

Use with "Soda Bottle Jack-o'-lanterns" on page 76.

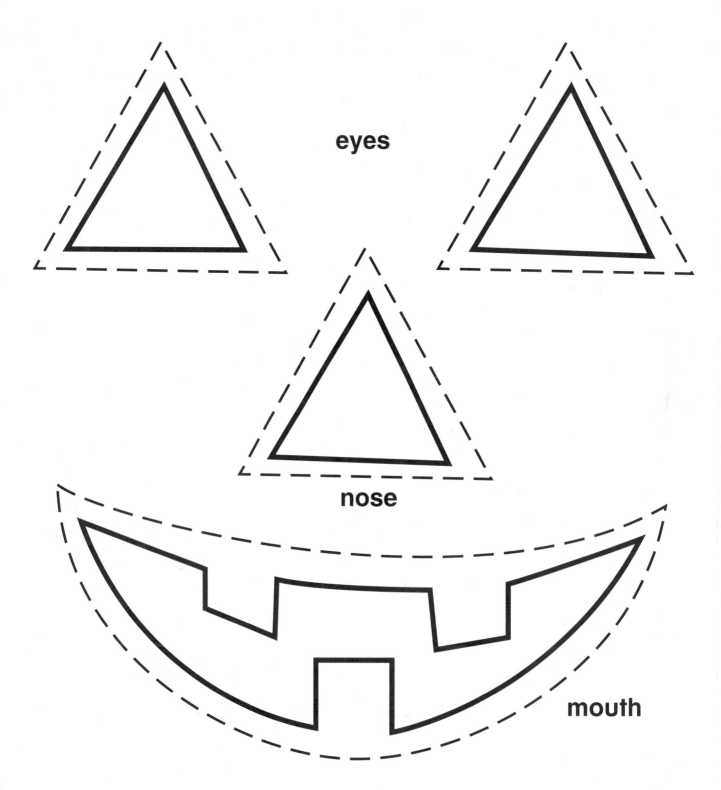

eyes

nose

mouth

Three Cheers for October PreK–K, SV 9829-9

Name _____

Pumpkin Puzzle

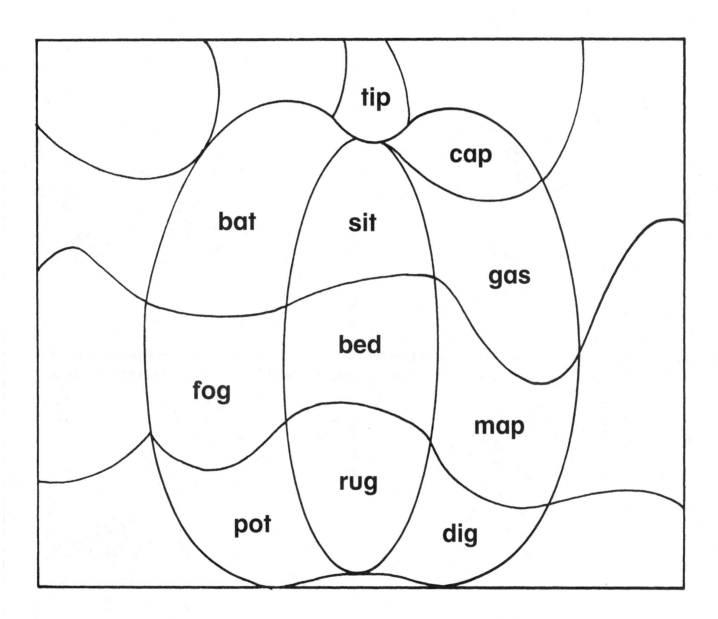

Directions: Use with "My Fat Pumpkin" on page 76. Invite children to read each word using onset/rime patterns. Have them color each section of the pumpkin orange and the stem green after they read the word. Have them color the blank sections blue.

Life Cycle Cards

Use with "From Seed to Pumpkin" on page 78.

Name _____

Describe the Pumpkin

The pumpkin is _____

_____

_____.

Directions: Use with "The Pumpkin Is . . ." on page 79. Have children look at the size, shape, color, and texture of the pumpkin. Have them write or dictate a word that describes the pumpkin to complete the sentence. Invite them to draw a picture of the pumpkin.

A Look at Eric Carle

 Eric Carle was born in Syracuse, New York, in 1929. He moved with his parents to Germany when he was six years old.

 He experienced many harsh times while growing up in Hitler's Germany. The teachers he had in school believed in physical punishment and made it difficult for him to enjoy learning.

 During this time, his father taught him to learn and sympathize with the creatures of the fields and forest. Carle developed a great love of nature which would be a definite influence in his stories later on.

 After the war, he attended and graduated from a prestigious art school in Stuttgart, Germany, where he learned graphic design.

 He had many happy childhood memories of living in America and had always wanted to return. So, in 1952 he moved to New York and began working as a graphic designer at *The New York Times*.

 The author Bill Martin, Jr., saw one of Eric Carle's drawings and asked him to illustrate his book *Brown Bear, Brown Bear, What Do You See?*

 Eric Carle then began to write his own stories, beginning with *1, 2, 3 to the Zoo*. It was soon followed by the celebrated classic, *The Very Hungry Caterpillar*.

 Since *The Very Hungry Caterpillar* was published in 1969, Eric Carle has written and/or illustrated over sixty books, many of which are award winners.

 The themes of his stories are drawn from his extensive knowledge and love of nature. He offers readers an opportunity to learn something about the world around them.

 His art is distinctive and instantly recognizable. He uses a collage technique with hand-painted papers which he cuts and layers to form bright and cheerful images. Many of his books have an added dimension such as die-cut pages or lifelike sounds.

Unit 7, Author Study: Teacher Information
Three Cheers for October PreK–K, SV 9829-9

The Very Busy Spider
by Eric Carle

A Collage Spider

Materials

- pattern on page 90
- white construction paper
- tissue paper (bright colors)
- scissors
- crayons
- paintbrush
- glue thinned with water

Directions

Teacher Preparation: Duplicate a copy of the spider on construction paper for each child. Cut tissue paper into small squares.

1. Look on the front cover of the book at the picture of the spider.

2. Glue tissue paper squares to completely cover the spider's body.

3. Gently paint over the spider with the thin glue to make the corners of the tissue paper stick.

4. Color the legs of the spider.

5. Cut out the spider.

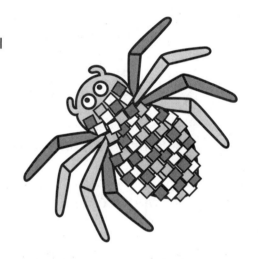

Spiders in the Webs

Materials

- activity master on page 91
- pencil
- crayons

Directions

Teacher Preparation: Duplicate a copy of the activity master for each child.

Invite children to draw lines to match the partner letters. Have them color the spiders.

Books by Eric Carle

■ *Do You Want to Be My Friend?* (HarperCollins)

■ *The Grouchy Ladybug* (HarperCollins)

■ *Have You Seen My Cat?* (Picture Book Studio)

■ *A House for Hermit Crab* (Picture Book Studio)

■ *1, 2, 3 to the Zoo* (Putnam Publishing)

■ *Pancakes, Pancakes* (Scholastic)

■ *Papa, Please Get the Moon for Me* (Picture Book Studio)

■ *The Tiny Seed* (Picture Book Studio)

■ *The Very Busy Spider* (Putnam Publishing)

■ *The Very Hungry Caterpillar* (Putnam Publishing)

■ *The Very Lonely Firefly* (Putnam Publishing)

■ *The Very Quiet Cricket* (Putnam Publishing)

Visit www.eric-carle.com for a complete list of books by Eric Carle.

Bookmark Patterns

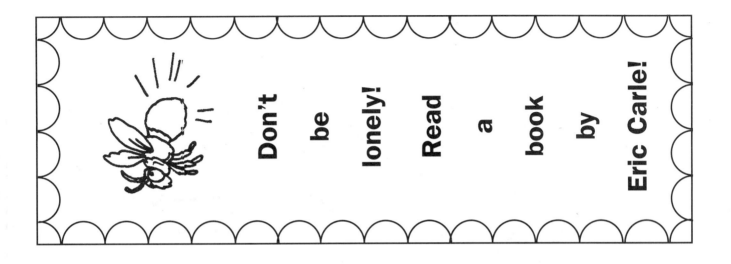

Don't be lonely! Read a book by Eric Carle!

Quietly read a book by Eric Carle.

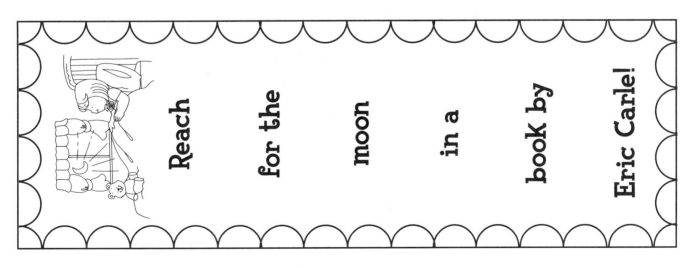

Reach for the moon in a book by Eric Carle!

Unit 7, Author Study: Patterns
Three Cheers for October PreK–K, SV 9829-9

Spider Pattern

Use with "A Collage Spider" on page 87.

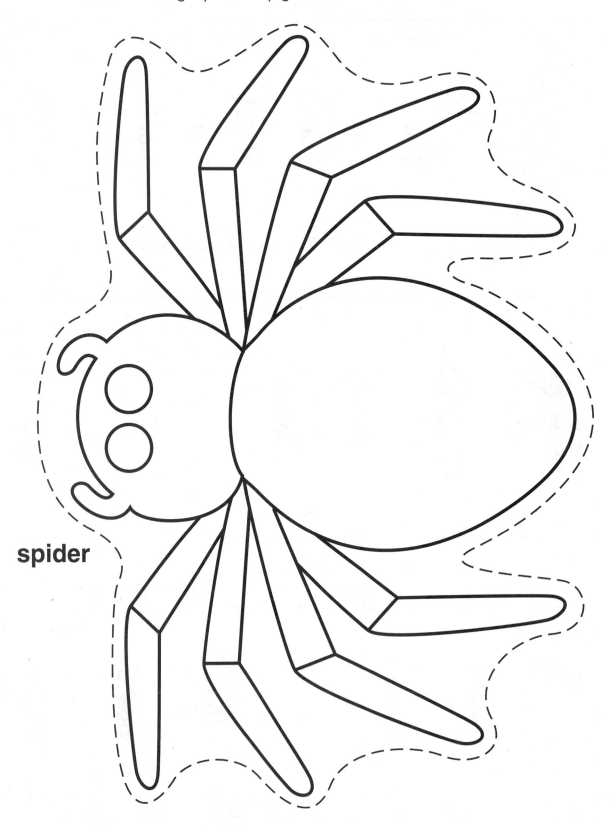

spider

Three Cheers for October PreK–K, SV 9829-9

Letter Match-up

Directions: Use with "Spiders in the Webs" on page 87. Invite children to draw lines to match the partner letters. Have them color the spiders.

Center Icons

Art Center

Dramatic Play Center

Block Center

Game Center

Three Cheers for October PreK–K, SV 9829-9

Center Icons

Language Center

Music Center

Math Center

Puzzle Center

Center Icons

Reading Center

Sensory Center

Science Center

Writing Center

Student Awards

Let's go "batty" over

_____

- - - - - - - - - - - - - - - - - -

_____ 's good behavior!

Child's name

_____   _____

Teacher's signature   **Date**

_____

- - - - - - - - - - - - - - - - - -

Congratulations, _____ .

Child's name

You are the October Student of the Month for

_____

- - - - - - - - - - - - - - - - - -

_____ .

_____   _____

Teacher's signature   **Date**

Student Awards Patterns
Three Cheers for October PreK–K, SV 9829-9

Student Award

Gotcha!

_____

_ _ _ _ _ _ _ _ _ _ _ _ _ _ _ _ _

_____ was caught

doing good work today!

_____   _____
Teacher's signature   **Date**

Calendar Day Pattern

Suggested Uses

- Reproduce one card for each day of the month. Write the numerals on each card and place it on your class calendar. Use cards to mark special days.
- Reproduce to make cards to use in word ladders or word walls.
- Reproduce to make cards and write a letter on each card. Children use the cards to form words.
- Reproduce to make cards to create matching or concentration games for students to use in activity centers. Choose from the following possible matching skills or create your own:
  - — uppercase and lowercase letters
  - — pictures of objects whose names rhyme, have the same beginning or ending sounds, contain short or long vowels
  - — pictures of adult animals and baby animals
  - — numerals and pictures of objects
  - — number words and numerals
  - — colors and shapes
  - — high-frequency sight words